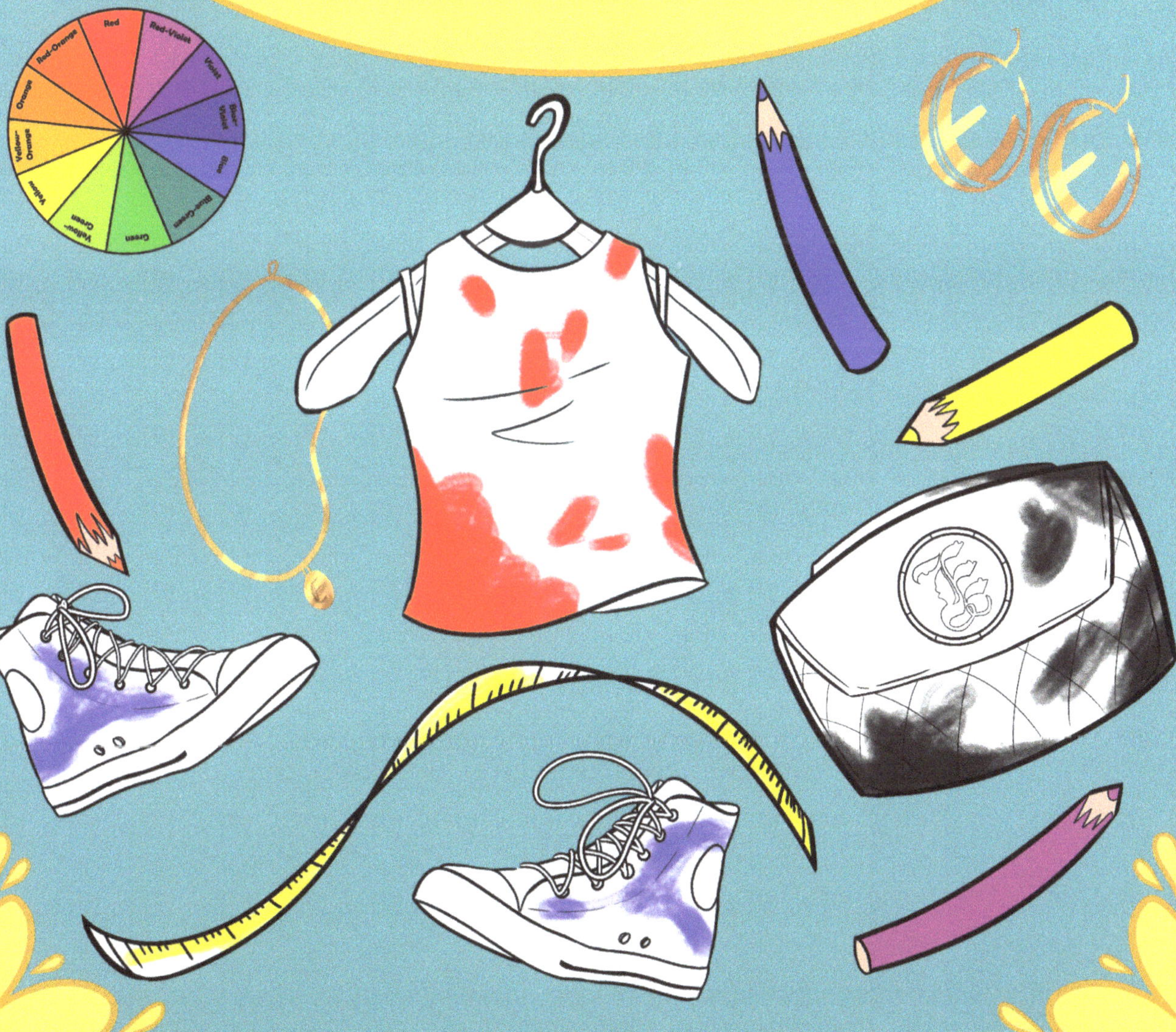

Emilydidit World
All Rights Reserved.
Copyright © 2022 Ebony Rice
v1.0

The opinions expressed in this manuscript are solely the opinions of the author and do not represent the opinions or thoughts of the publisher. The author has represented and warranted full ownership and/or legal right to publish all the materials in this book.

This book may not be reproduced, transmitted, or stored in whole or in part by any means, including graphic, electronic, or mechanical without the express written consent of the publisher except in the case of brief quotations embodied in critical articles and reviews.

Outskirts Press, Inc.
http://www.outskirtspress.com

ISBN: 978-1-9772-5416-0

Cover and Interior Art © 2022 Mindie Armas. All rights reserved - used with permission.

Outskirts Press and the "OP" logo are trademarks belonging to Outskirts Press, Inc.

PRINTED IN THE UNITED STATES OF AMERICA

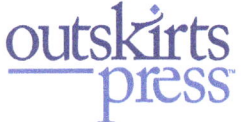

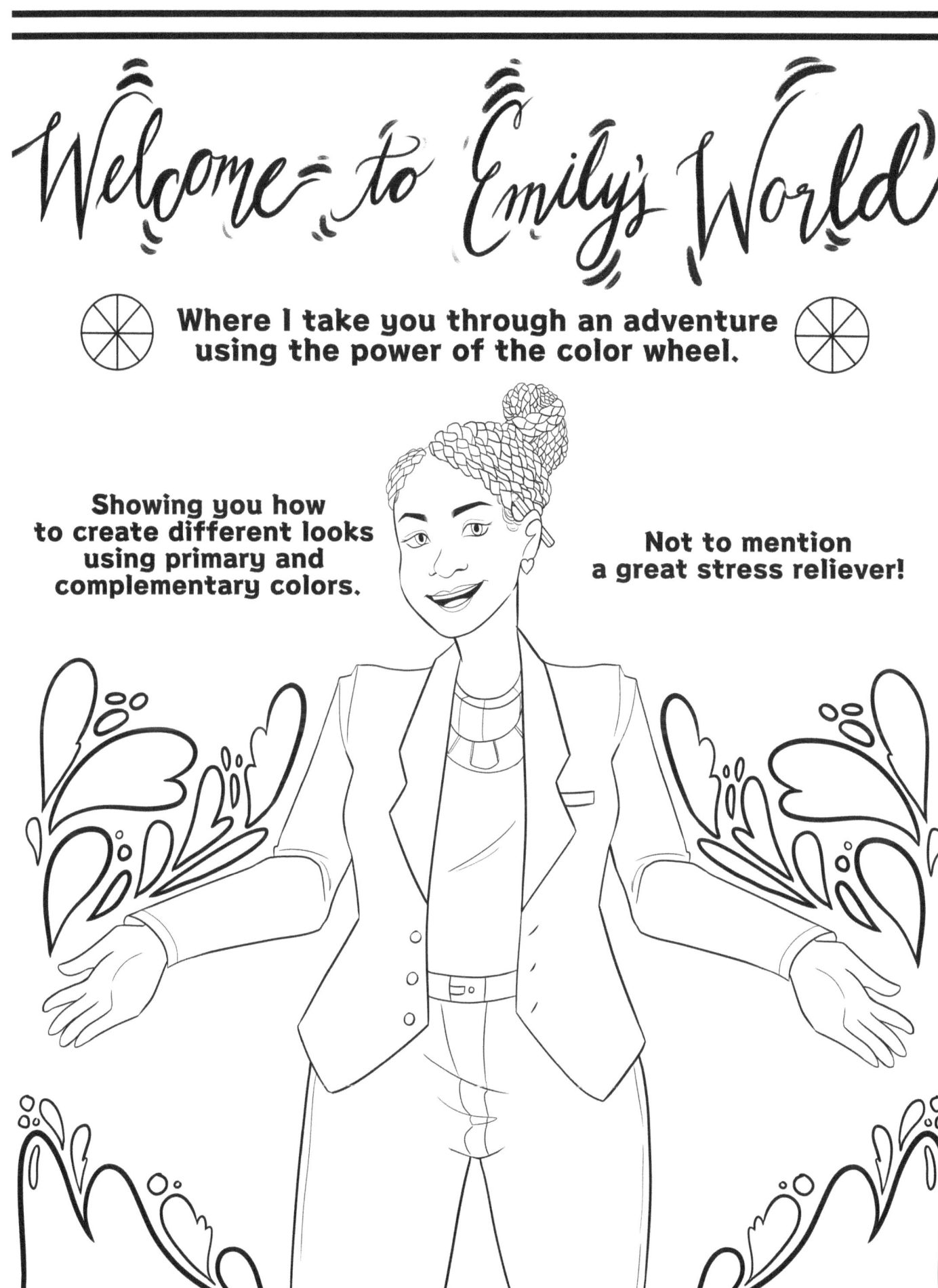

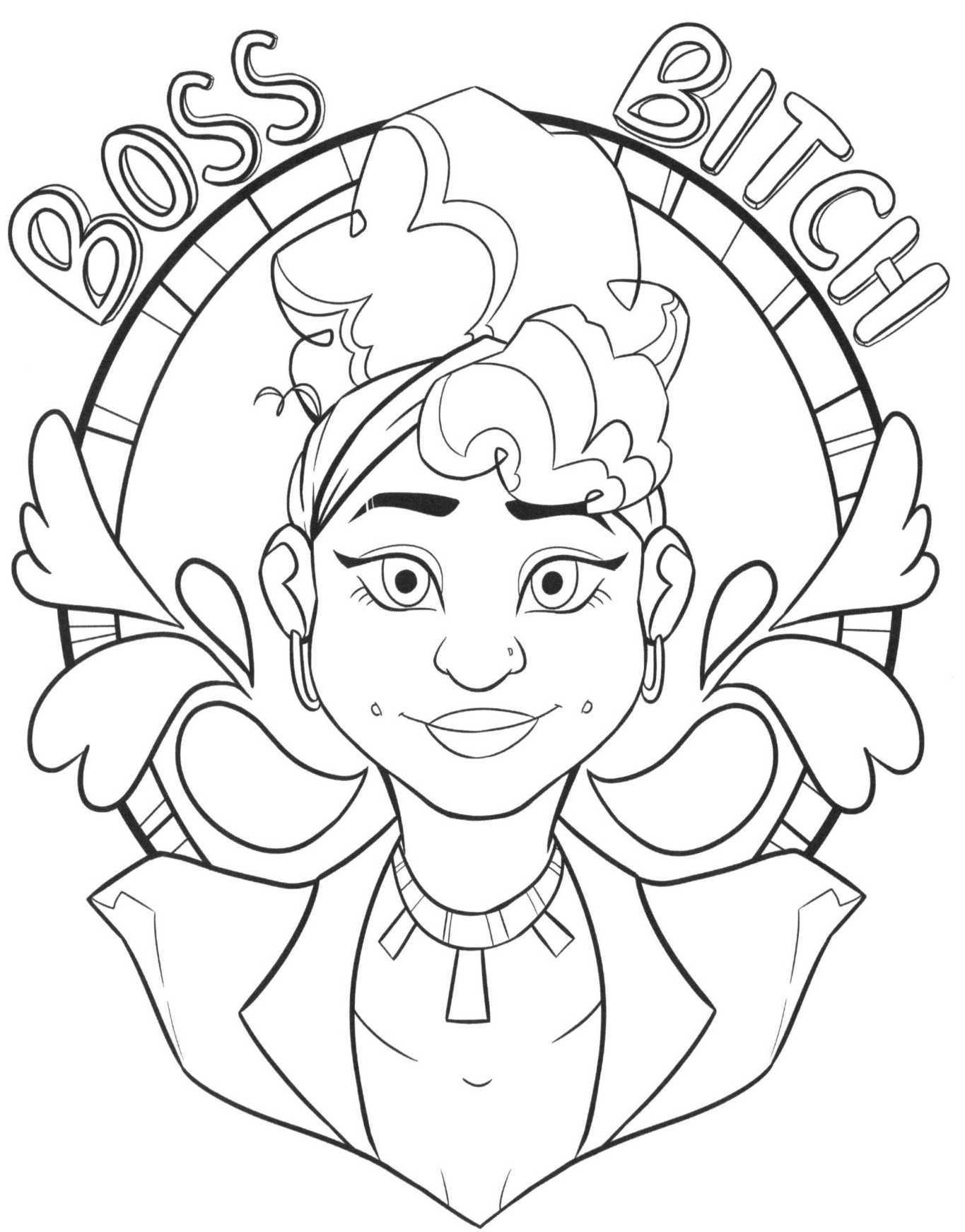

Lesson 1:

Learn to create, not hate

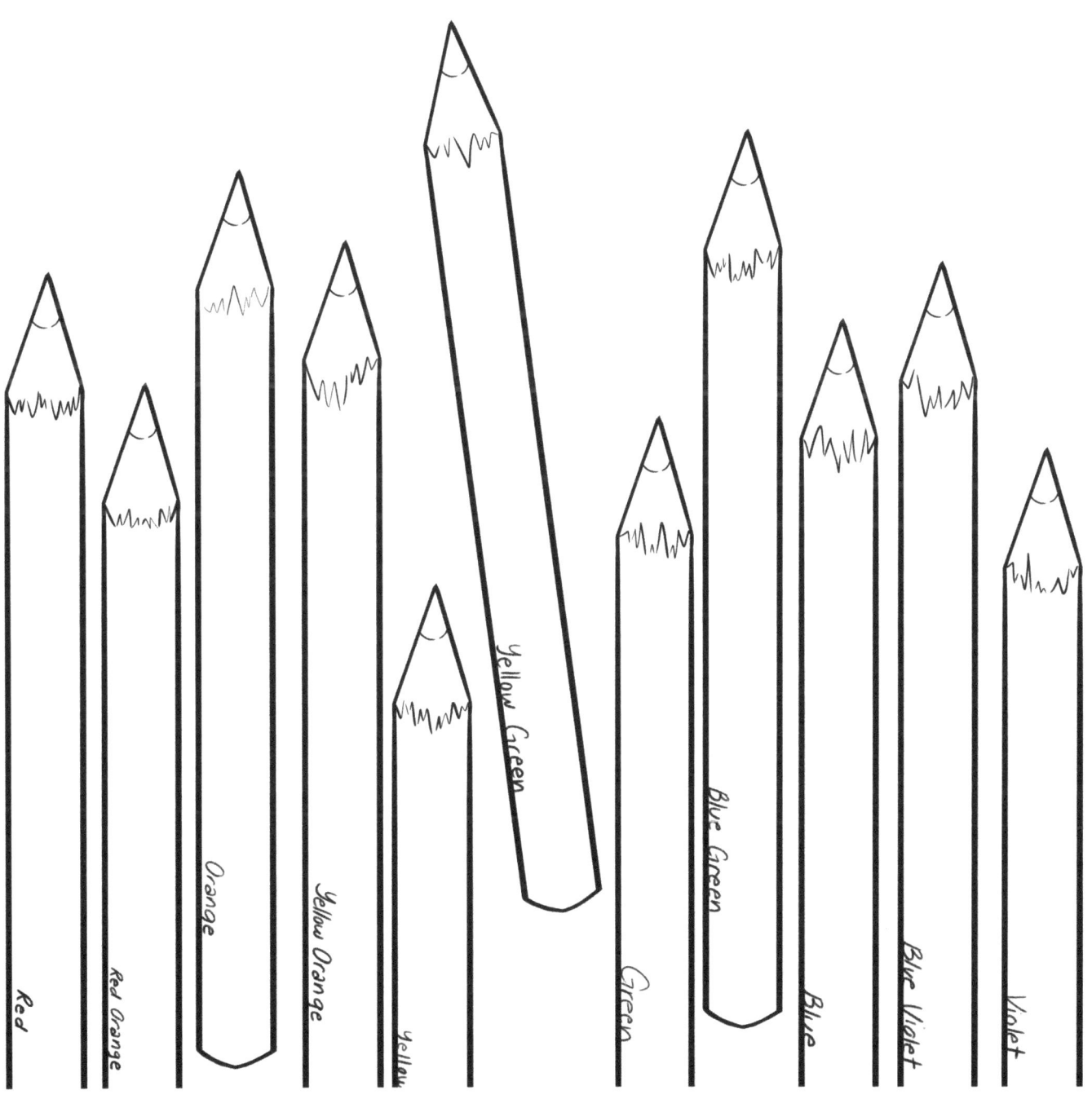

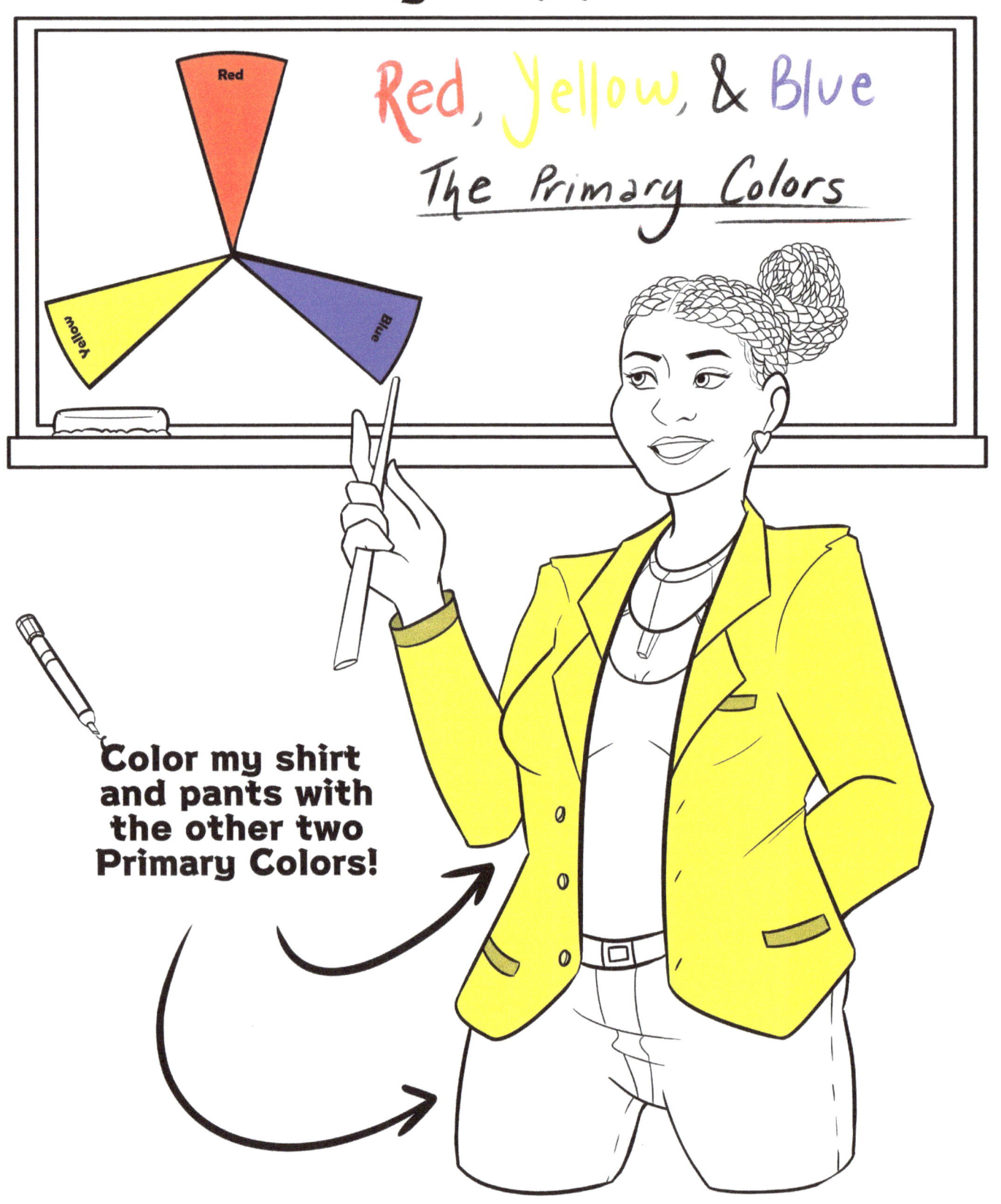

**If its blue it might be for you
or yellow who is the lucky fella
but red might go straight to your head.**

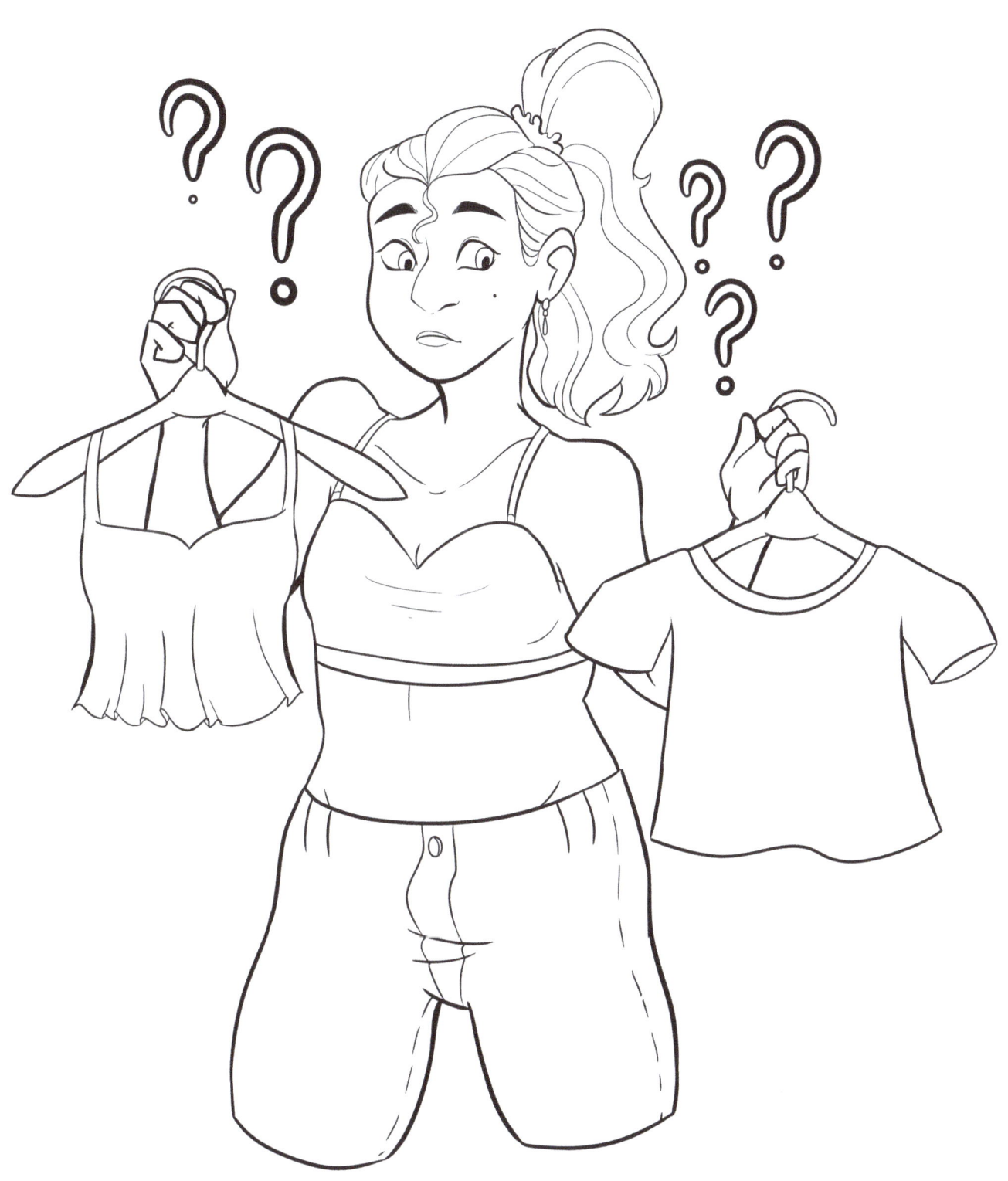

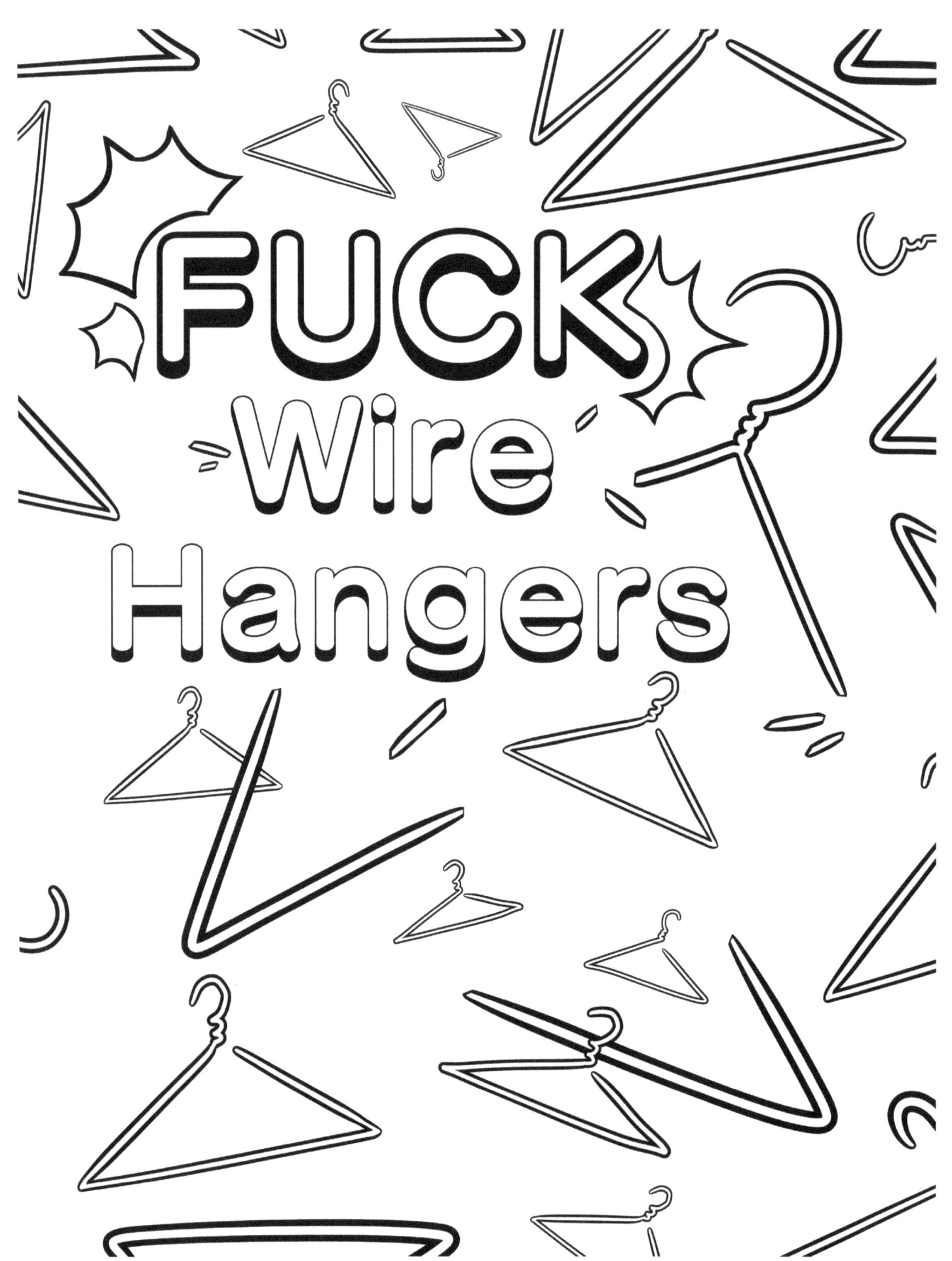

Lesson 2:
Complement my primary

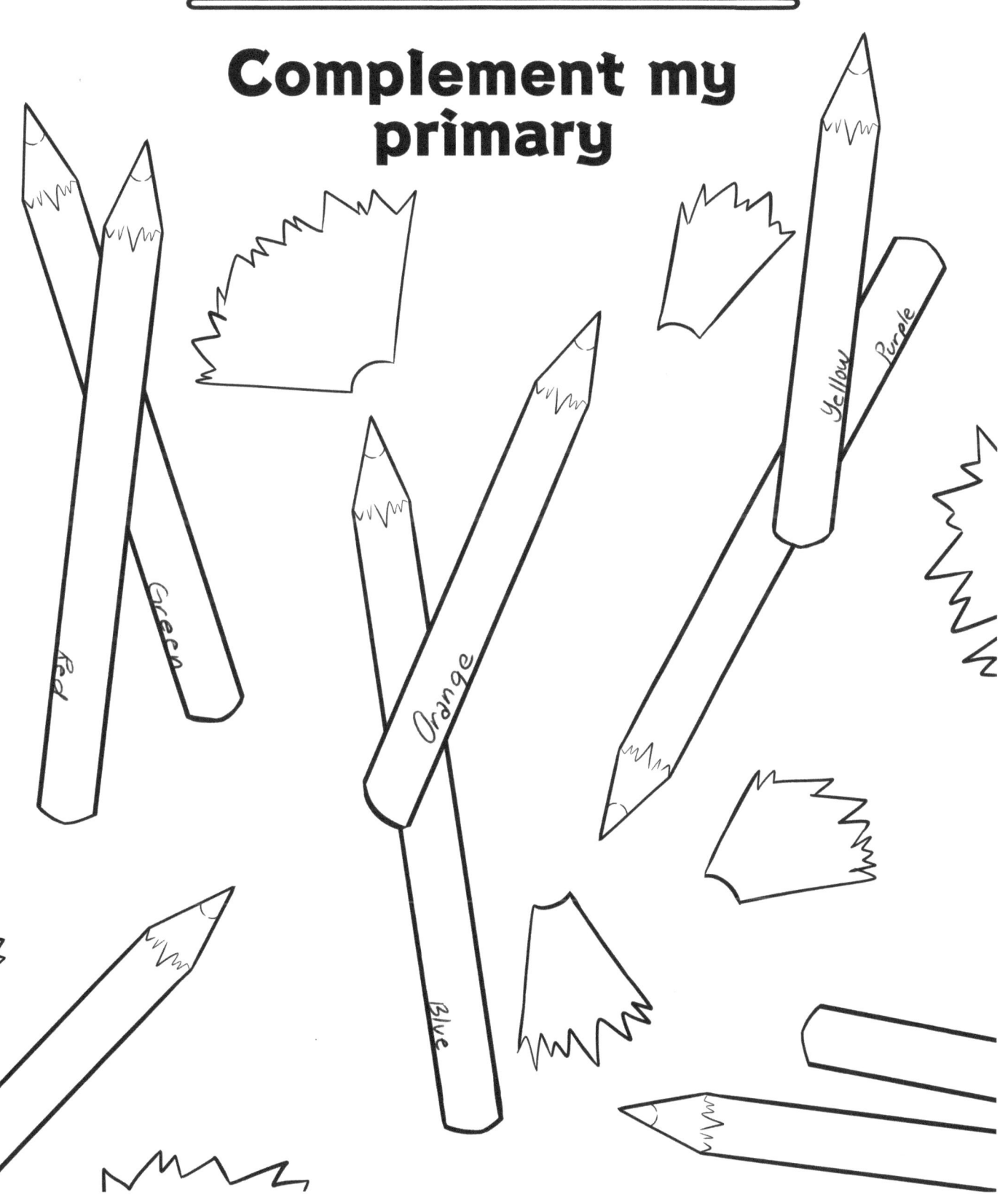

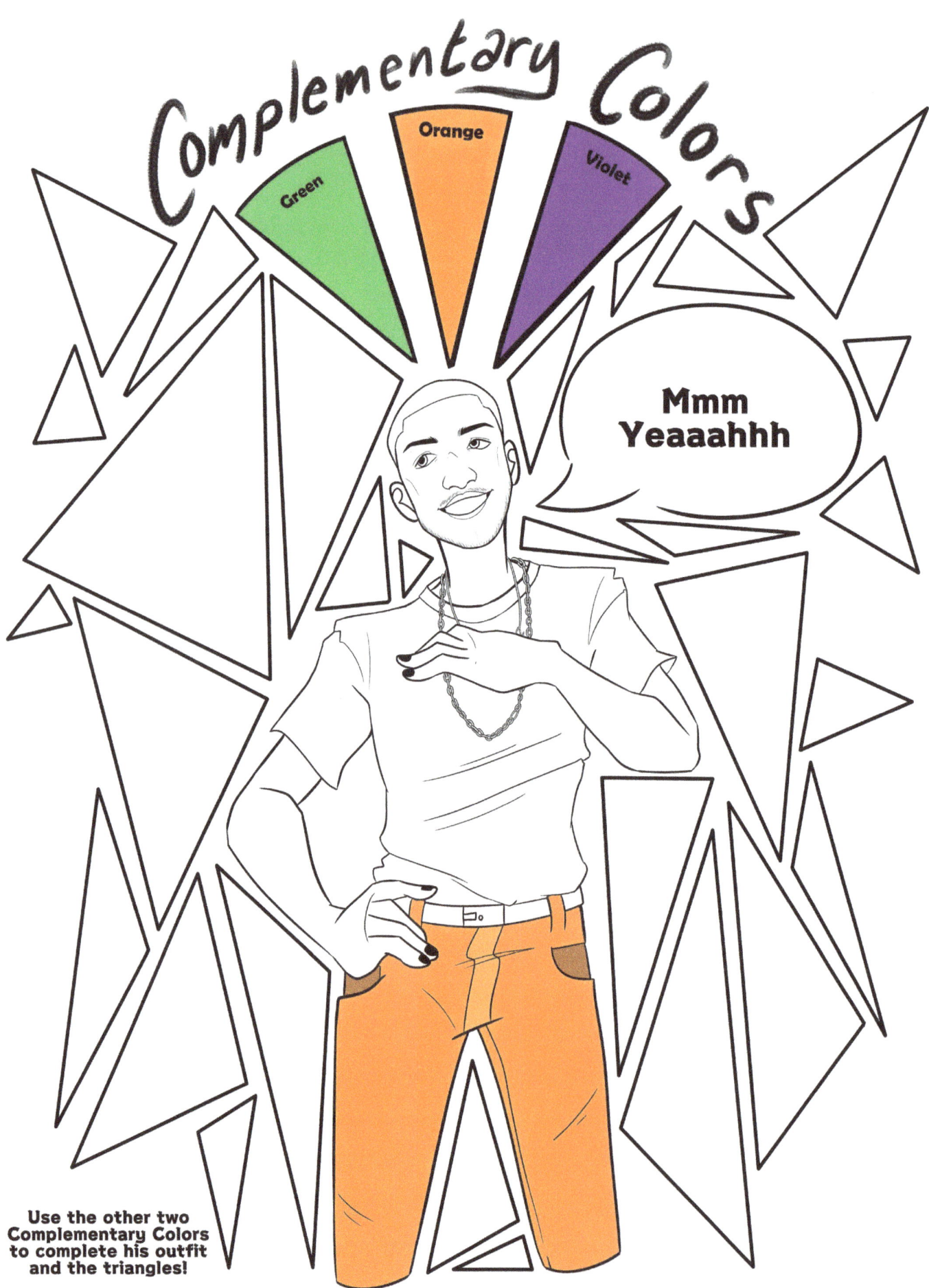

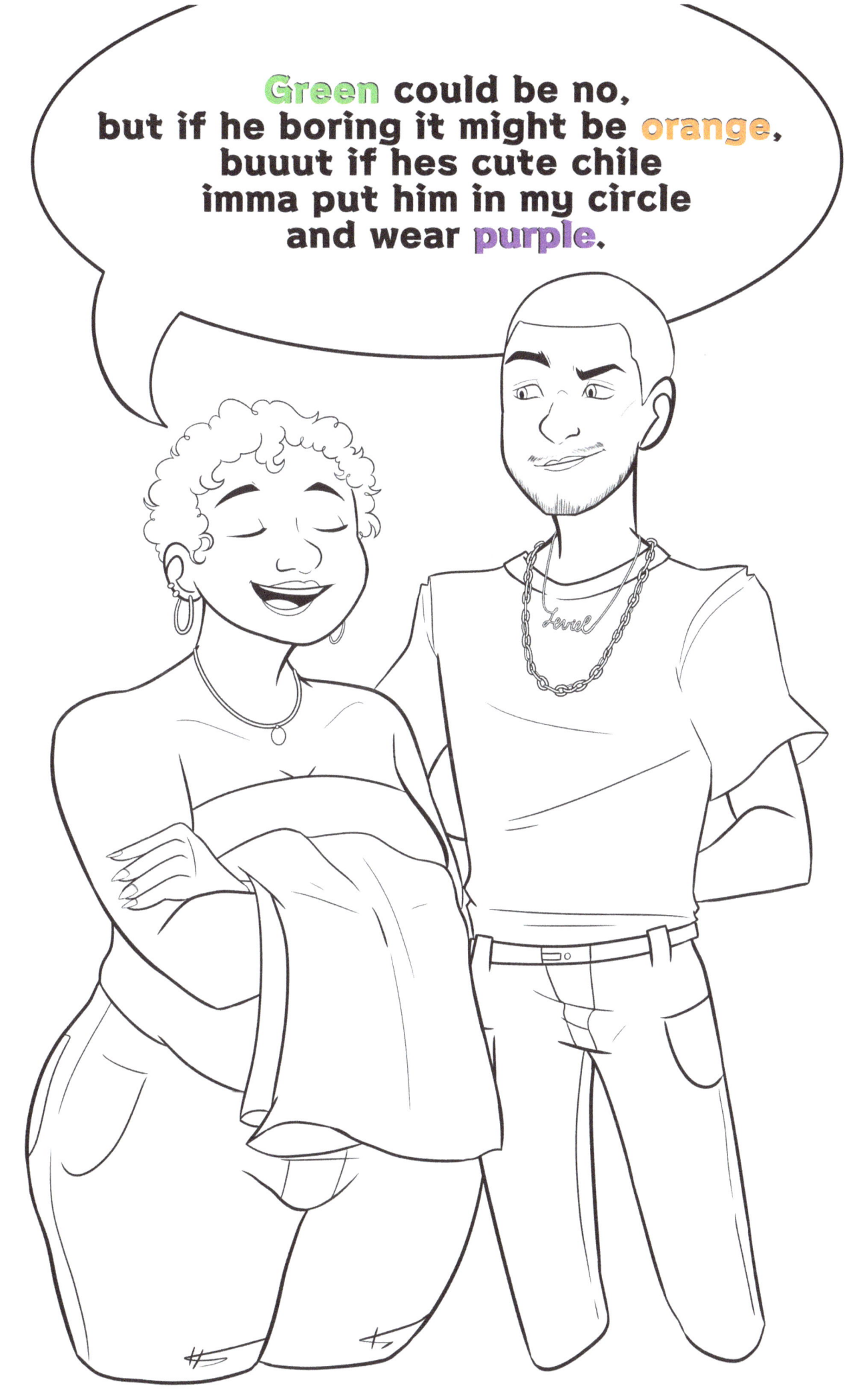

Now it's your turn!
Create a look using the Primary and Complementary colors.

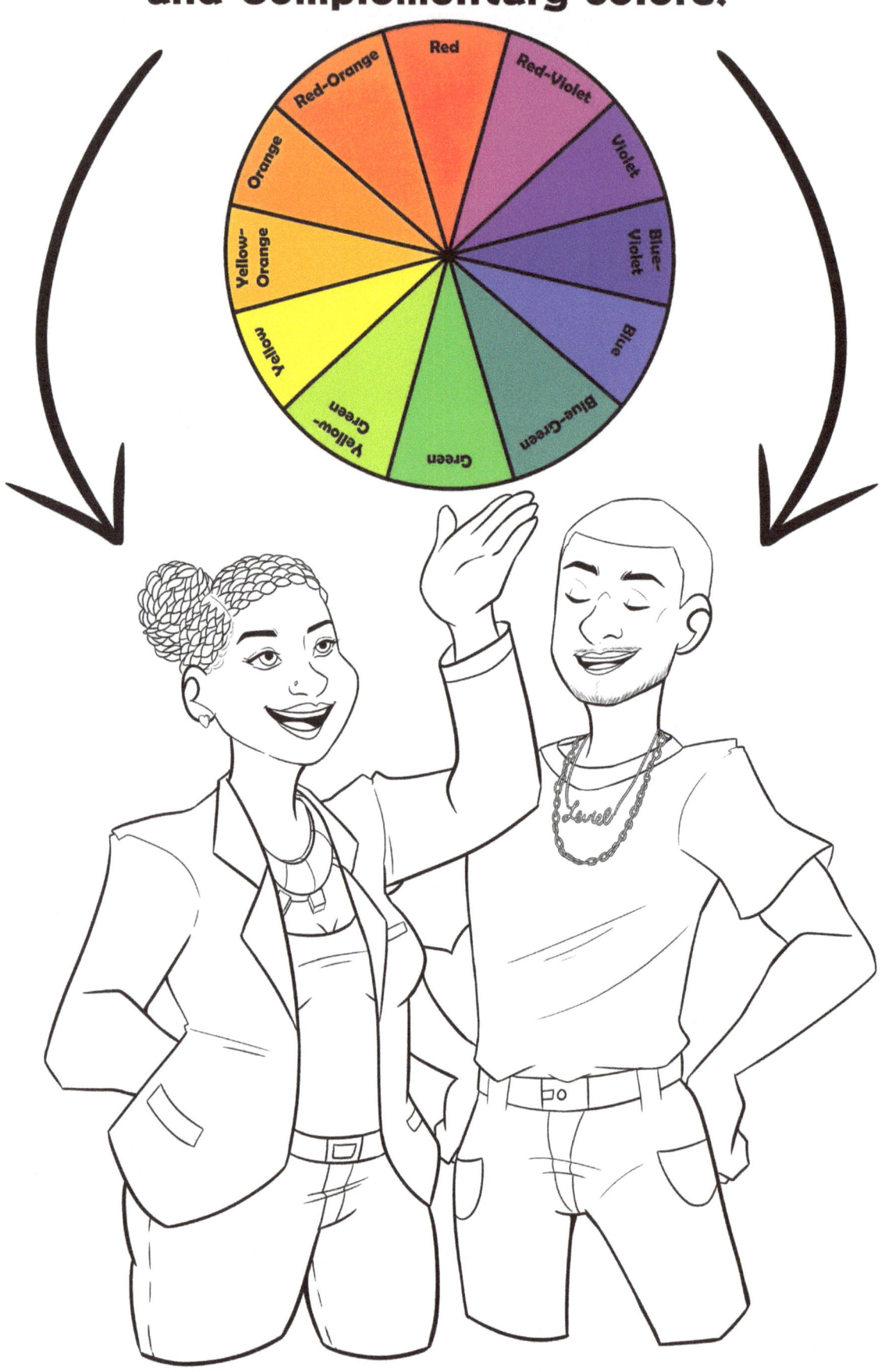

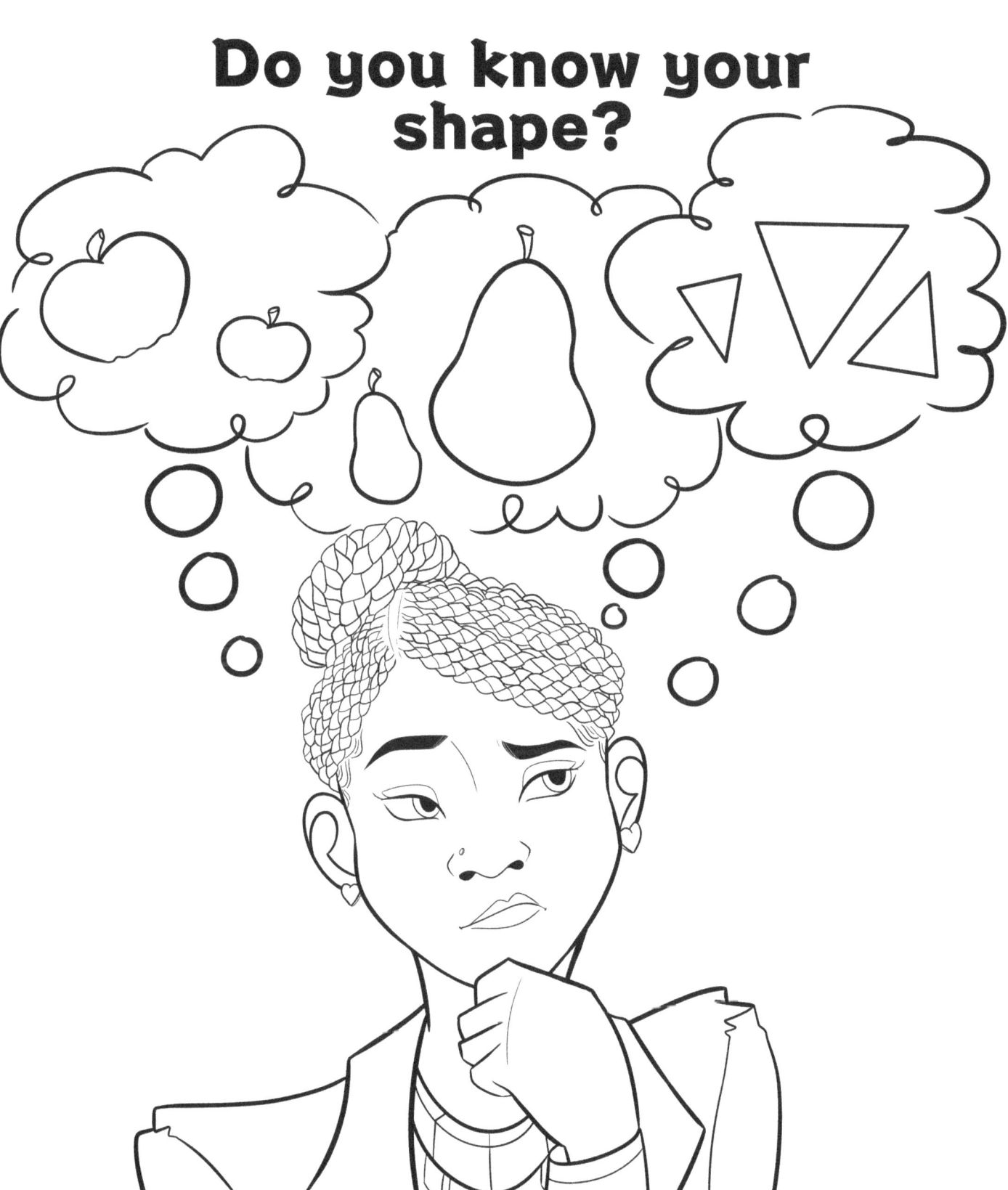

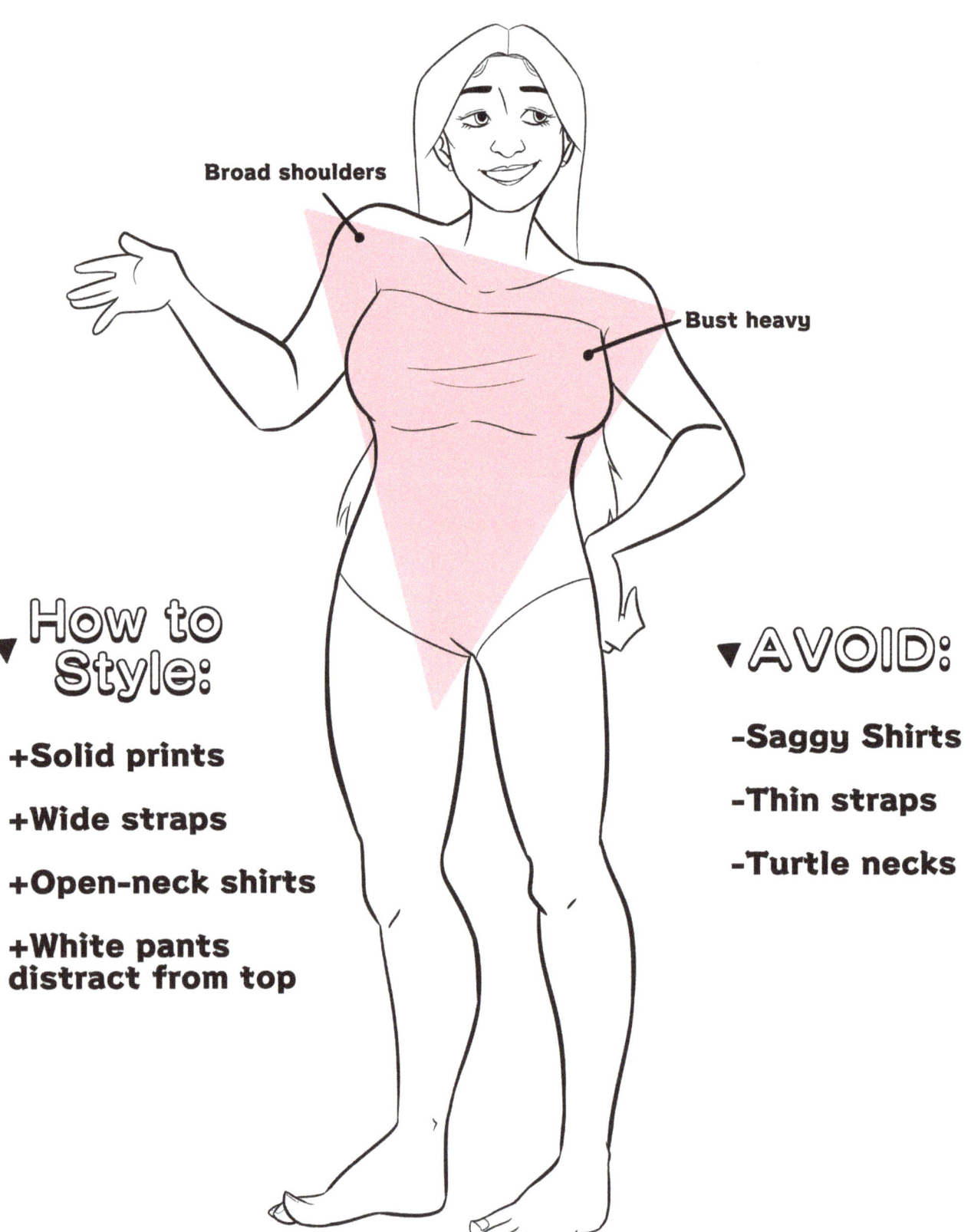

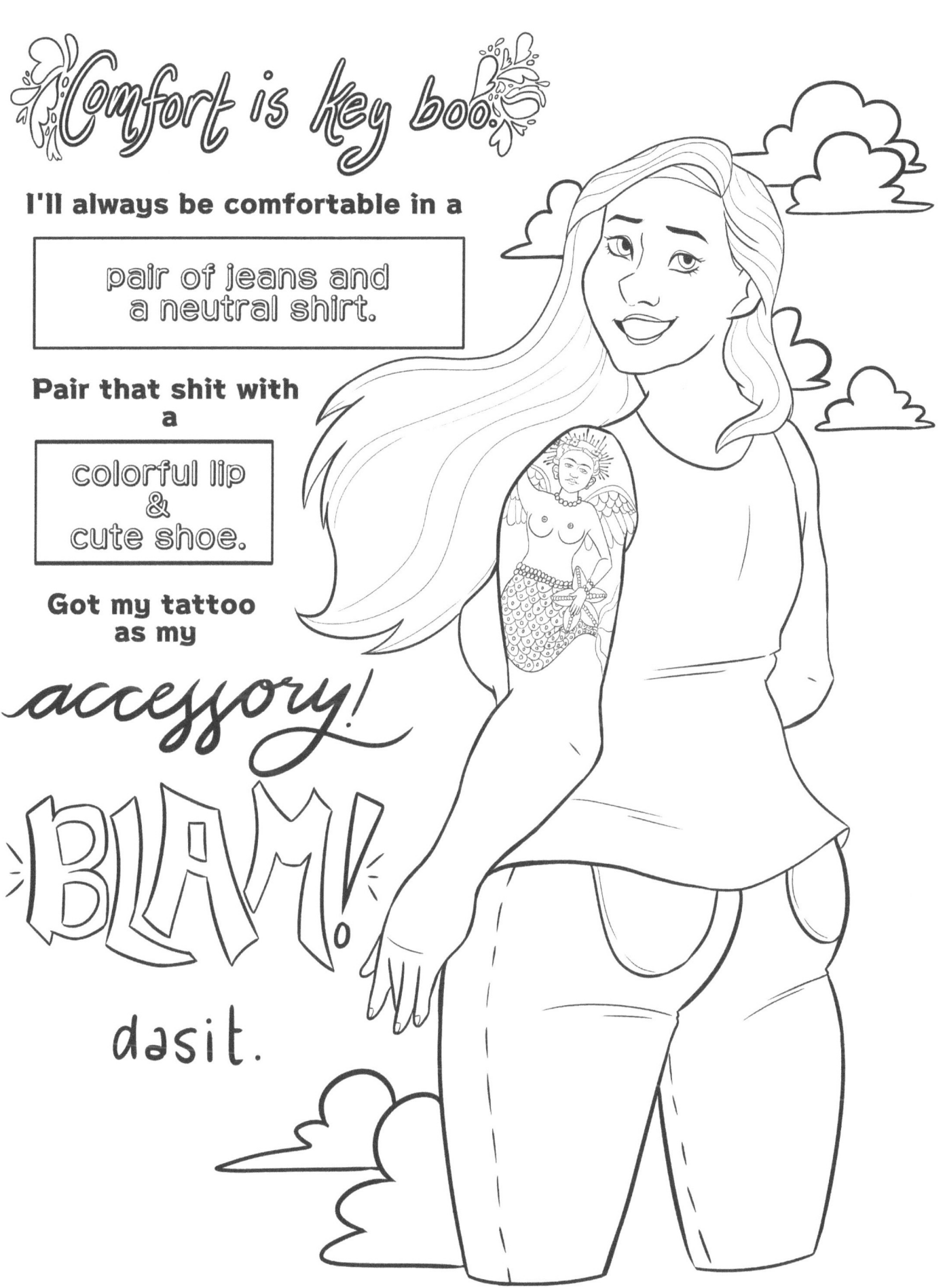

Apple

How to Style:

+ Trouser cut jeans *wider/flare
+ Wedge/pointy toe shoe
+ Belts (wide)
+ wrap dress

AVOID:

- Skinny jeans
- Leggings
- Tube dresses
- Round toe shoes

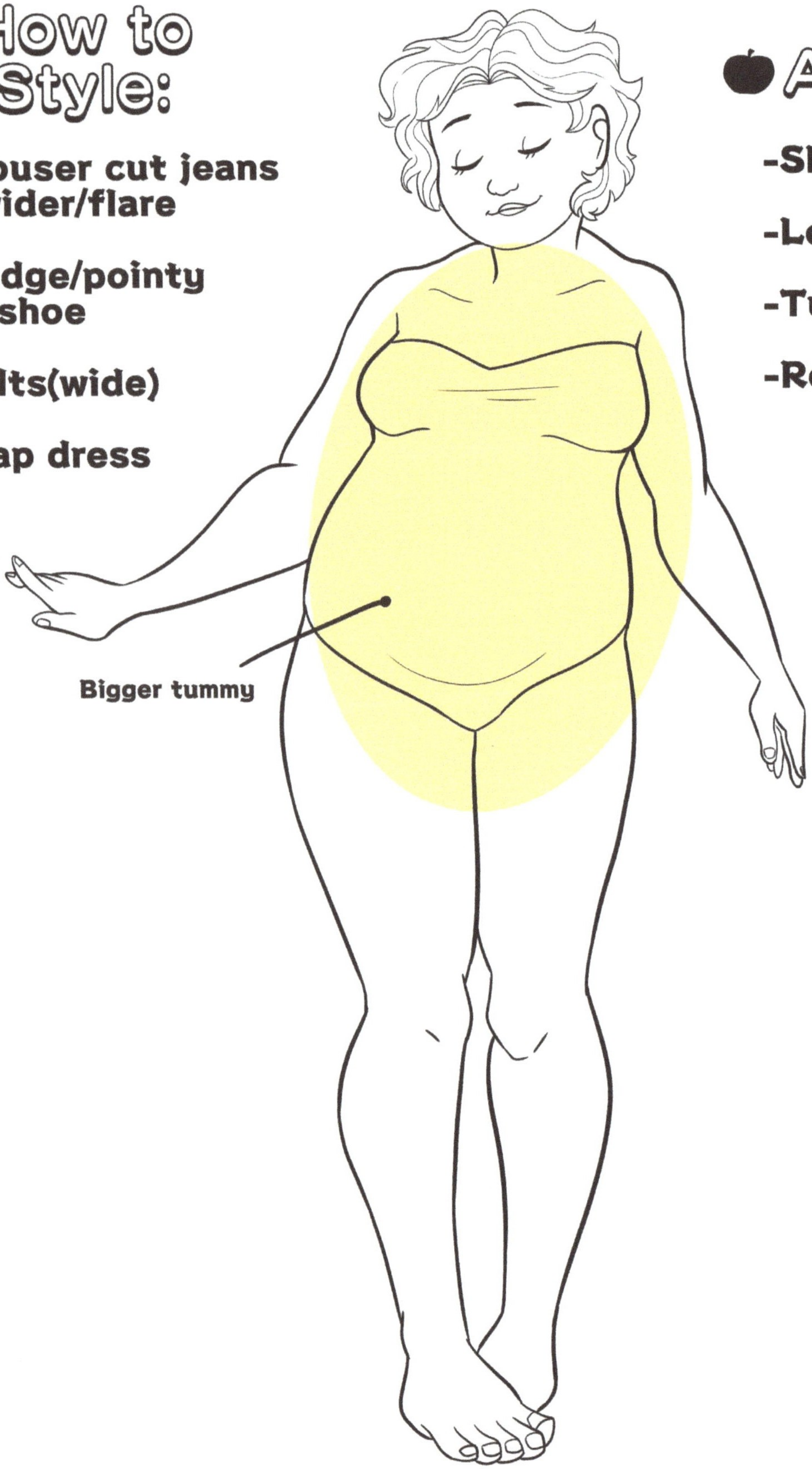

Bigger tummy

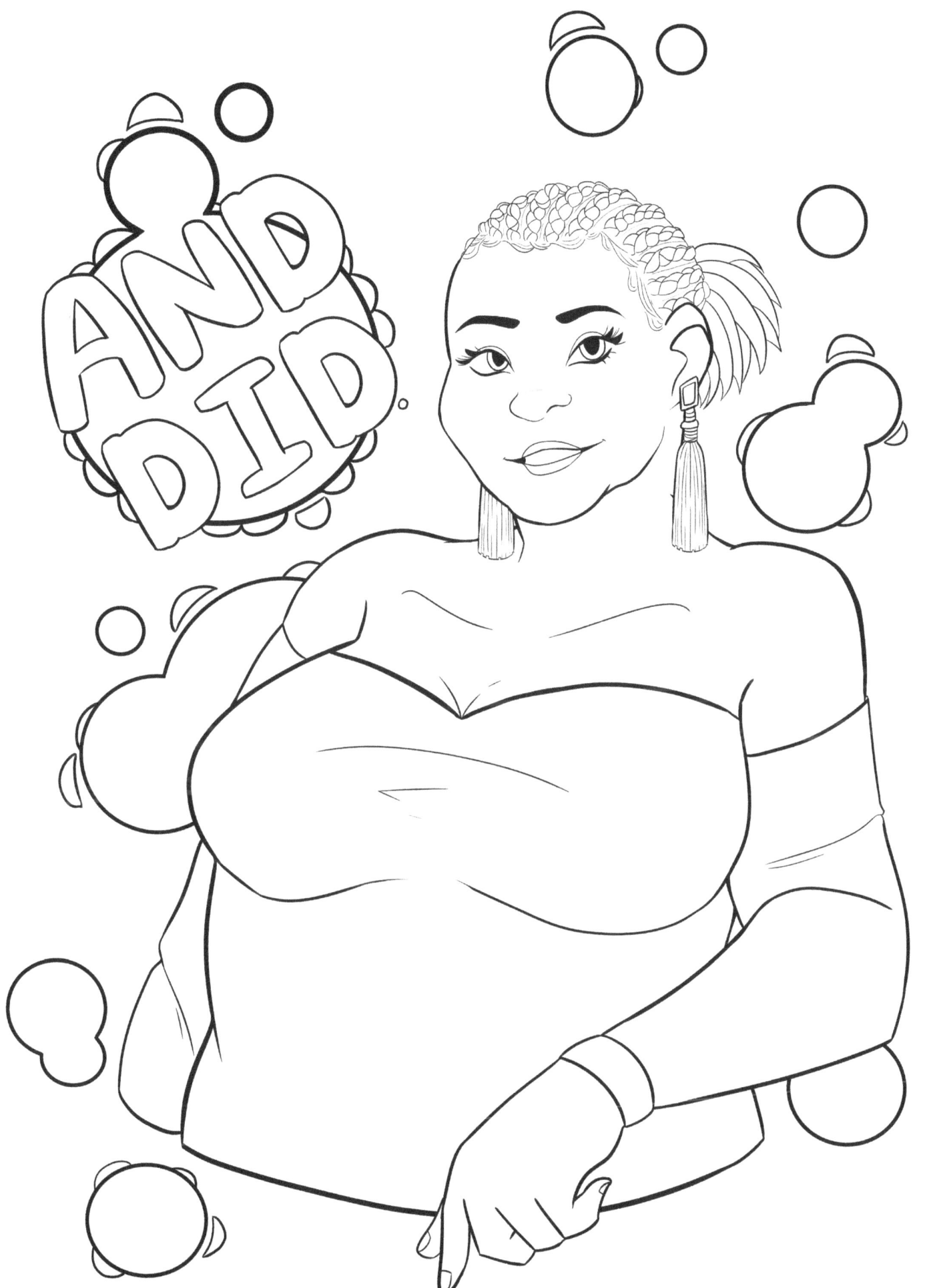

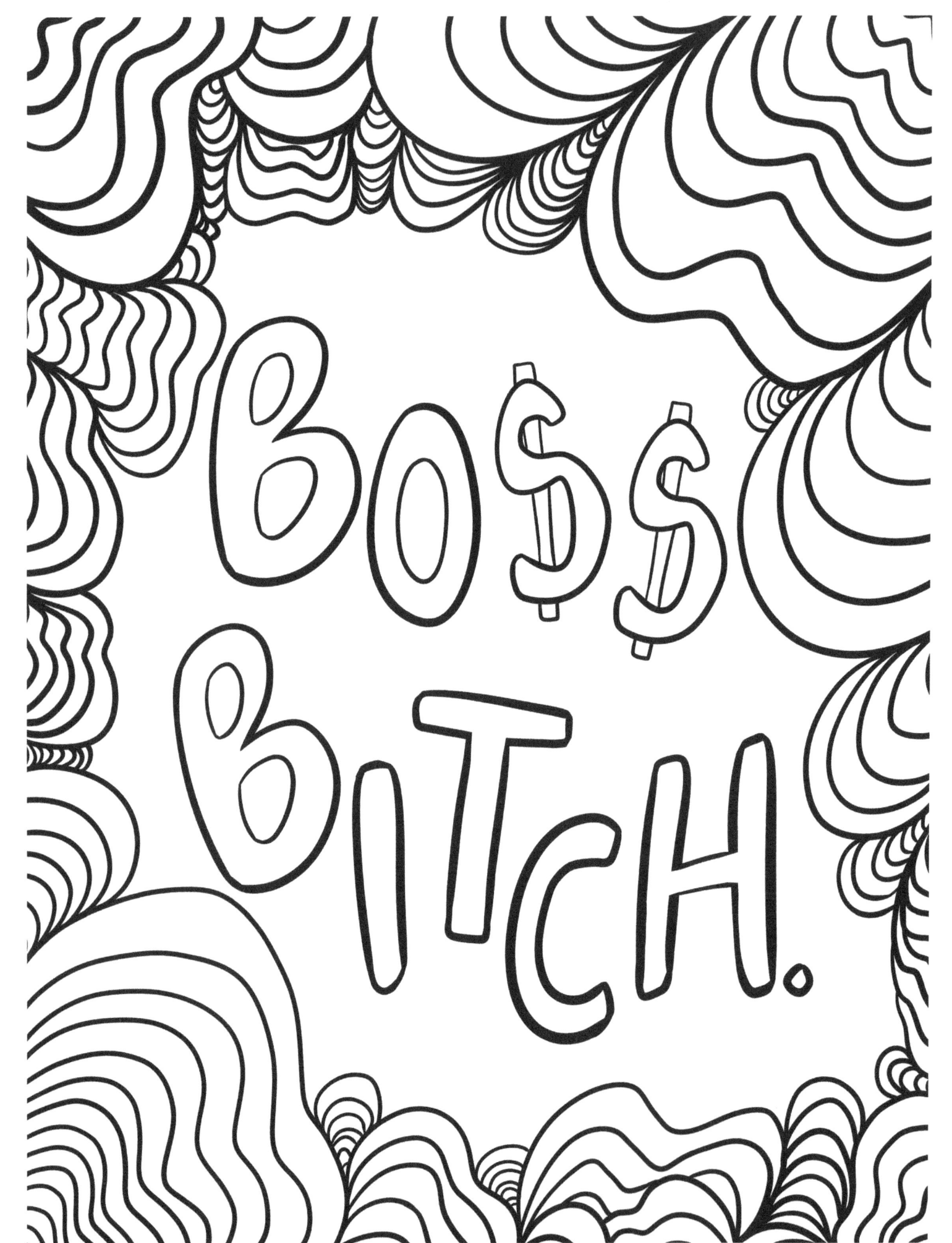

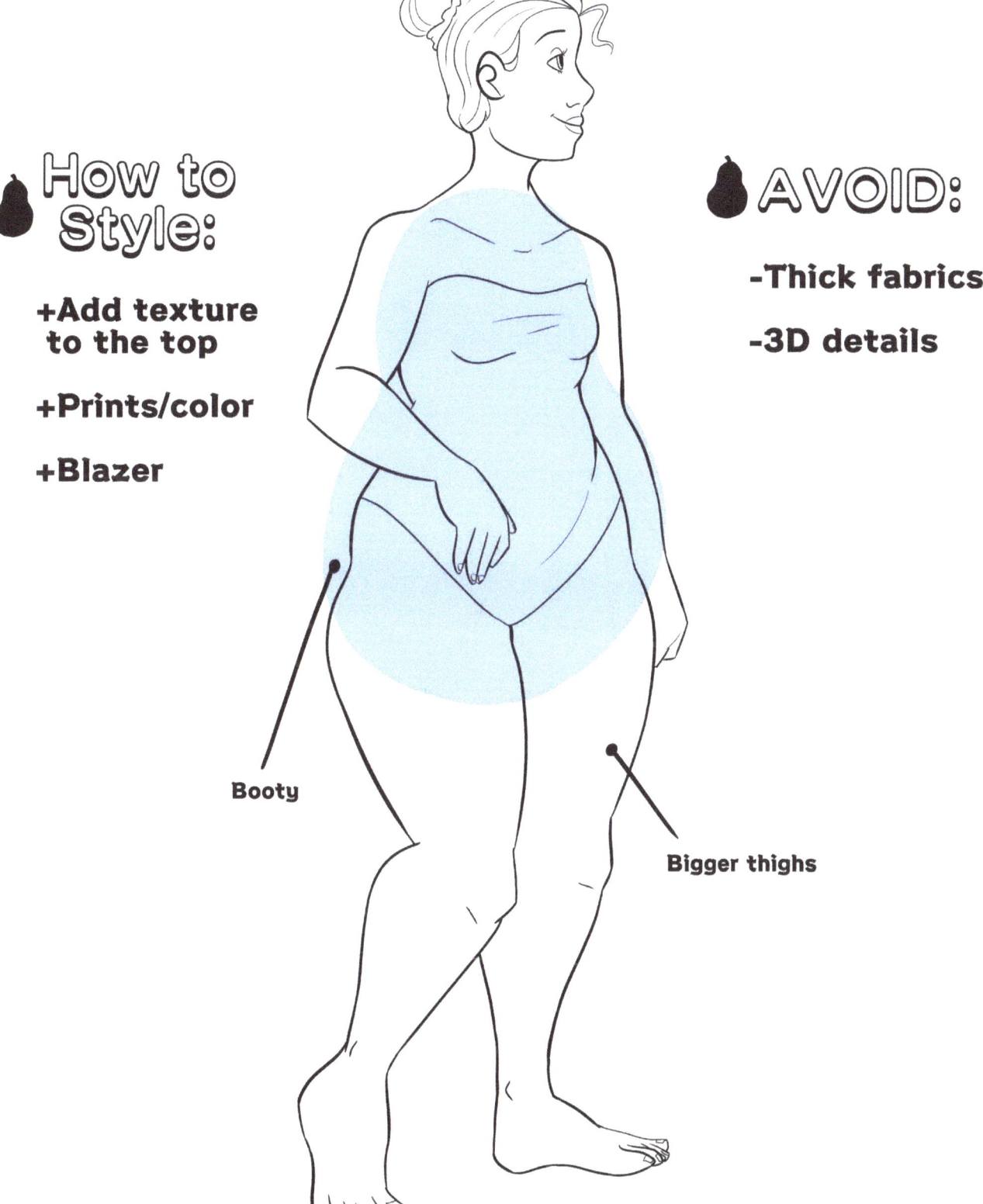

Pear

How to Style:
+Add texture to the top

+Prints/color

+Blazer

AVOID:
-Thick fabrics

-3D details

Booty

Bigger thighs

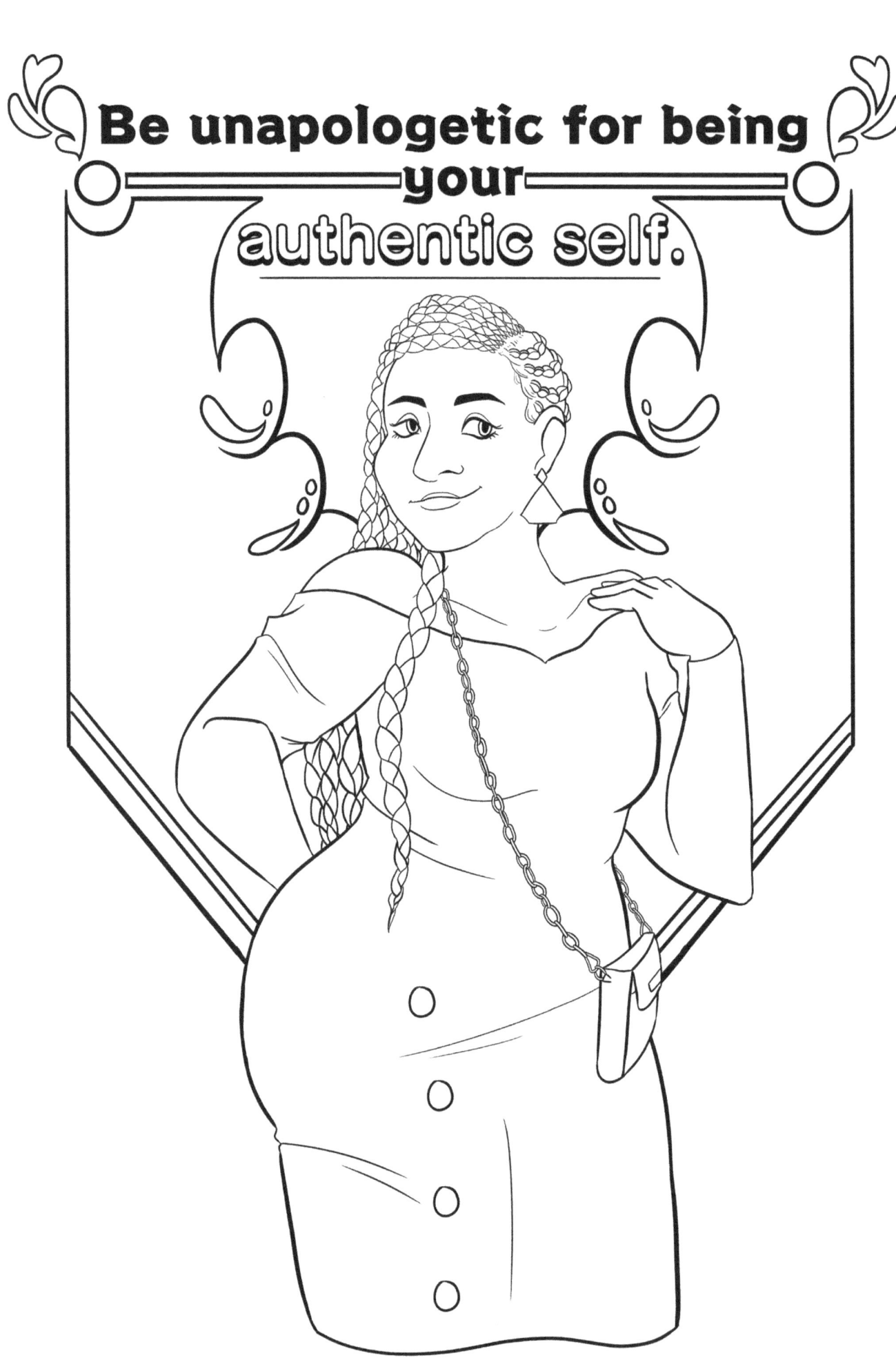

Lesson 4:

Style is figuring out what works for you and your body type.

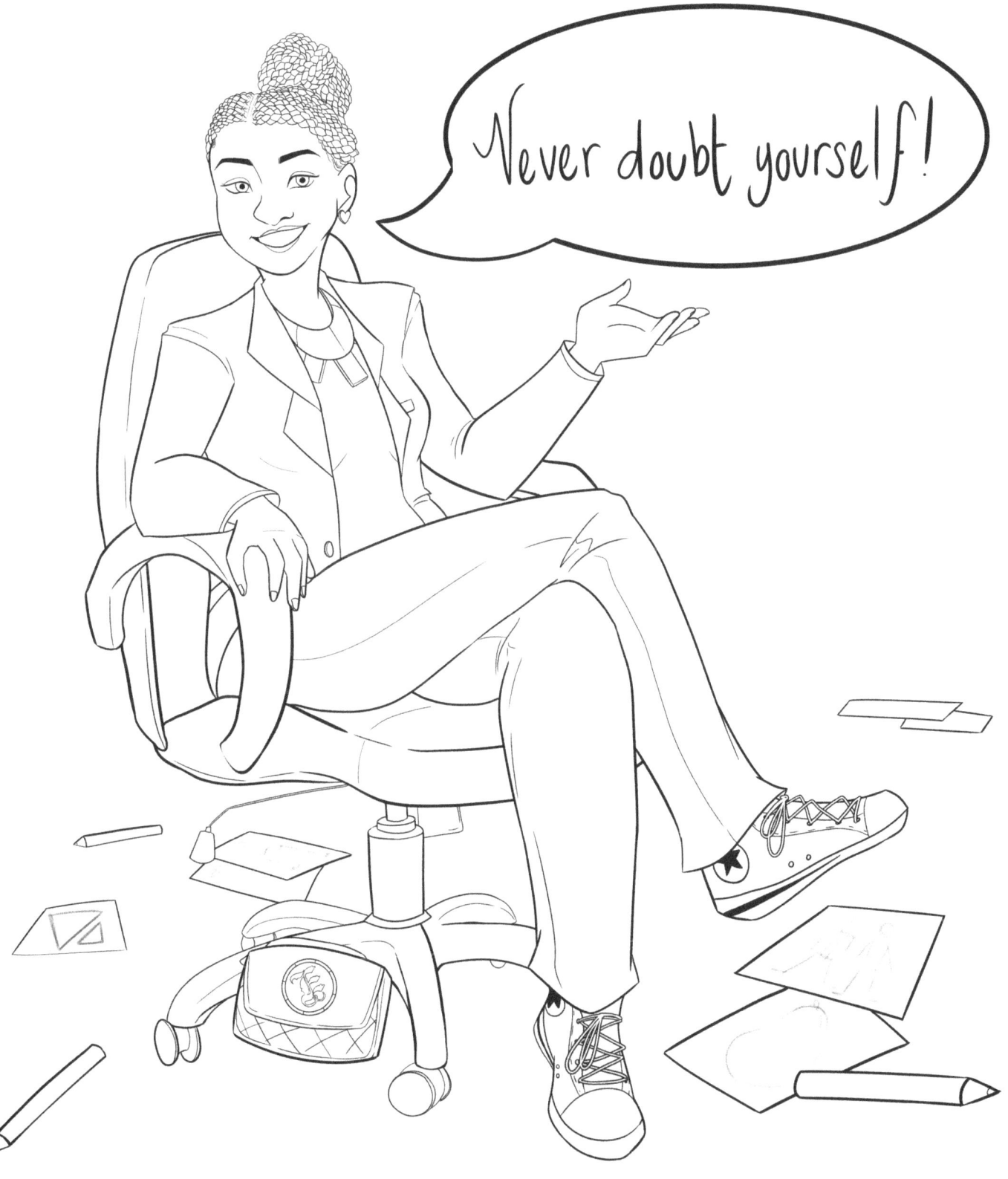

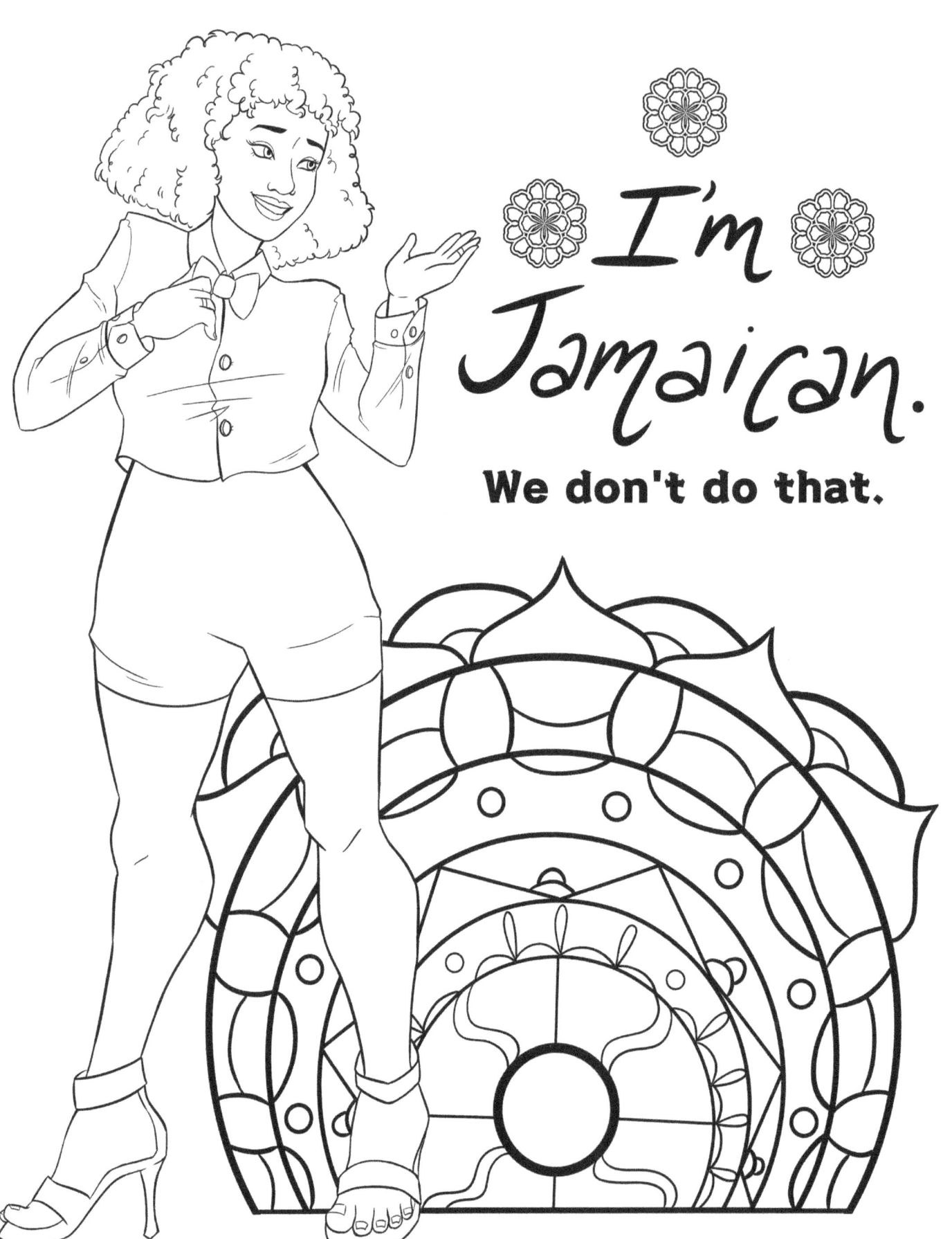

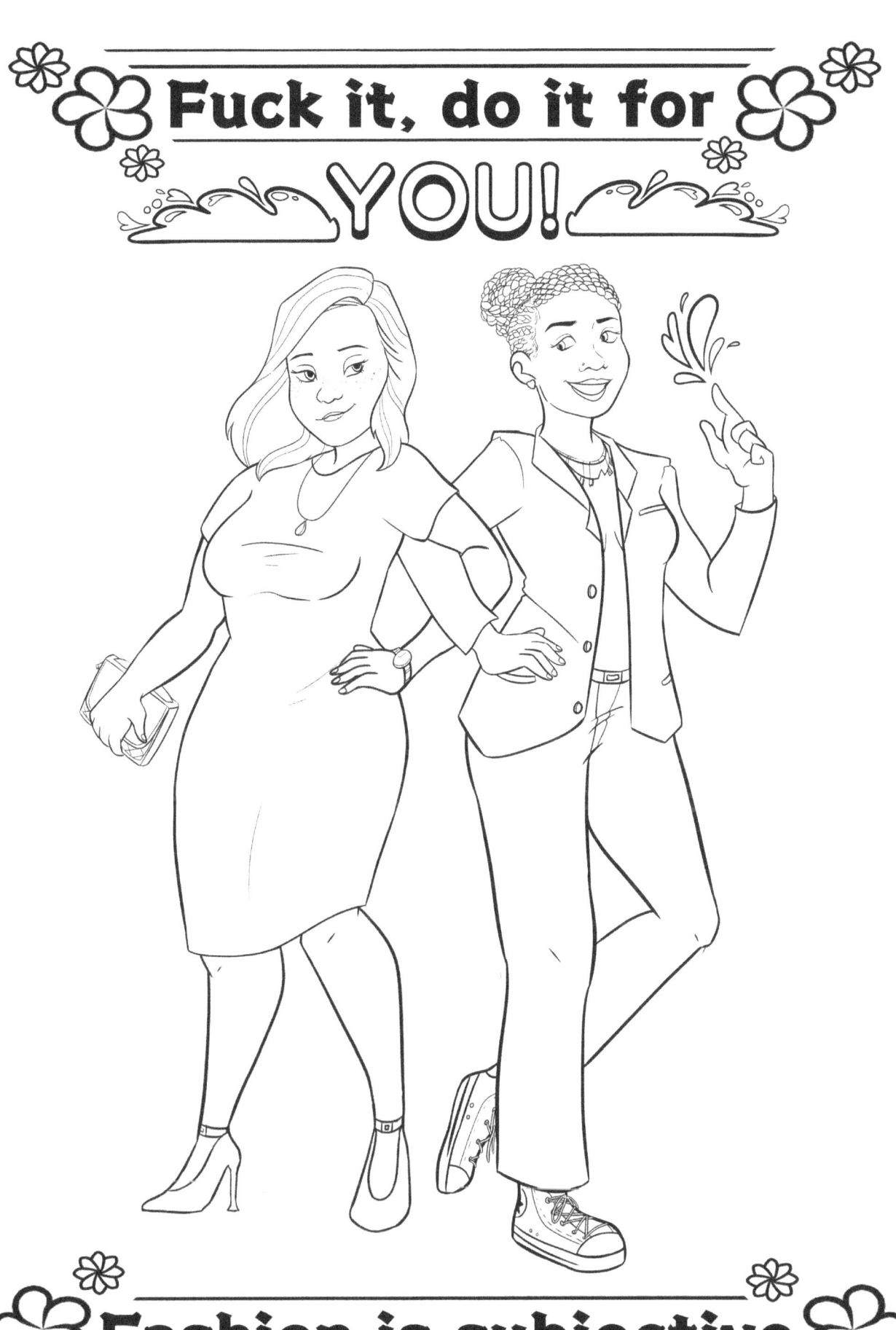

Dedication

I dedicate this book to my spirit animal.
My left and right side of my brain. The person
who reminds me every other day who the fuck i am...

Tyreece Allen Jr.

Also where would I be in life without my girls.
If the word "support" had a group photo,
it would show

Jessica J. Felt, Ayesha Rogers,
Dr. Kimberly Harris, Dr. Mercedes A. Shuler &
Shaneka Johnson.

www.ingramcontent.com/pod-product-compliance
Lightning Source LLC
Chambersburg PA
CBHW040545220526
45473CB00016B/3024